The Epitaph

Sierra Hinzman

BookLeaf Publishing

India | USA | UK

The Epitaph © 2024 Sierra Hinzman

All rights reserved.

No part of this publication may be
reproduced, stored in a retrieval system, or
transmitted, in any form or by any means,
electronic, mechanical, photocopying,
recording or otherwise, without the prior
written permission of the presenters.

Sierra Hinzman asserts the moral right to be
identified as author of this work.

Presentation by *BookLeaf Publishing*

Web: www.bookleafpub.com

E-mail: info@bookleafpub.com

ISBN: 9789363310698

First edition 2024

*For tomorrow, may you be empowered by this
today*

Wishes

I close my eyes and feel the dreams flood my
mind,
Bittersweet reality ties me to my pillow,
Ice-cold sheets sting my back,
And all I can do is breathe for a wish.

I toss and I turn restless in the starlight,
My eyes open to the room darkened by
midnight,
As my heart flies by moonlight,
But all I can do is dream of a wish.

I create white noise that numbs me to sleep,
But even my mind cannot be contained in a
dream,
As I am once more thrusted into consciousness,
All I can do is hope for a wish.

A wish.

A penny in the currency of dreams.
A token for all the things that could be.

A wish.
I wish on the starlight,

The midnight,
The moonlight.
A wish.
I wish on the sunrise,
The sunset,
The twilight.
So, weave into my heart,
The O so sweet wishes,
Weave into my heartbeat,
The rhythm of hope.

Weave into my tears an essence of change,
The strength to face trials,
The strength to walk away.

Weave into my soul the ability to love
For without it, I might not be able to wish,
Wish that I could say "I love you".
Weave me into my wishes,
Weave me into hope,
Weave me into courage and love.

For when I wish, I know the starlight shines a
little brighter,

And I can only wish that my life might shine as
bright, in this world of darkness.

Crossroads

Here we are at a crossroads,
And I choose to go,
And you will go on as you did when I left
before,
And I will go on and find something more.

Goodbye is a language I wish we didn't speak
into existence.
What is this?
Reminiscent of a time we weren't these ages,
In cages?

Here we are at a crossroads,
And I choose to go,
And you will go on as you did when I left
before,
And I will go on and find something more.

Trapped by a crime that keeps us locked
together,
Like mercury rain in a bitter-cold December.
It's not you it's me will not be our epitaph,
We were something so good for too long to write
that.

Here we are at a crossroads,
And I choose to go,
And you will go on as you did when I left
before,
And I will go on and find something more.

Yes, I will grieve you,
Be bound by this goodbye.
A language we once had never imagined,
When we started.

A truth tomorrow echoes for the departed.
A summer new beginning for my heart and,
A chance to mend the pieces, you already
started.

Moving On

I think the hardest part of moving on is the guilt
for choosing to put yourself first, and the talk
from others as if you fail to realise your impact
on their lives.

I think the hardest part of moving on is not
blaming yourself for how you choose what's
best for you, even if it might change things for
others.

Your change means their change.
Your comfort means their discomfort.

And all the while you try to justify staying in a
situation where you reap little benefit and are
mistreated consistently.

I think the hardest part of leaving is them not
knowing why. You wouldn't do that to them the
way they did it to you.

You won't go behind their back to spill their
dirty laundry on everyone else's floor in an
attempt to justify your innocence.

You won't stoop to their level though they have
made your standards bend to theirs.

You are stuck between staying silent or speaking
- and in both you will be the bad guy so you
choose the former to maintain a sense of
decency in your dissent.

I think the hardest part of leaving is facing
yourself, seeing yourself for who you are and
not who they have turned you into.

Seeing yourself as beautiful, strong, and
confident - not afraid of the truth and not afraid
of your truth.

Not afraid of waking and not afraid of sleeping.

The hardest part is finding that spark, that
dreamer, that person who could find the beauty
and see the beauty and hold the beauty of day in
her eyes.

Goodbye, dare I say is not the hardest,
It is in the waiting to accept goodbye.
For once the time to say goodbye arrives,
The heart is mended enough to look forward
again.

What If

I closed my eyes to embrace the wind in my hair,
To feel the sun on my skin,
To hold a piece of me again.

For my eyes breathe reality into my body.
A present I wish to pass,
A future I wish to hold,
Bidding tomorrow to stay at last.

Tapping on the window of time,
Begging the door to open wide,
Knowing it takes but a second in life to change,
Knowing most seconds strive to remain the
same.

But what if I want it?
What if I want out?
Amicably departed.
Rhetorically restarted.
But what if I want it?
What if I want out?
More than just a fleeting thought.

A need not a simple want.

But what if I need it?
What if I need out?
It takes a moment for the door to open.
And a miracle to cross its threshold.
The enemy of change is the notion of prosperity
in the lies we tell ourselves to cope with the
present.

In the lies we confuse needs with wants.
We say it's selfish to want it.
It's selfish to want out.
But what if I need it?
What if I need out?

Lighthouse

I left my hometown to find you,
My lighthouse in the sea.
I thought you'd be my solitude,
But you were a tsunami.

I thought I'd leave the ghosts behind,
That my mind could finally be free,
But you took my new beginning,
Pretending you were remedy.

You took the streets I called home,
Making them seem distant.
And when I brought concerns to you,
You would look away resistant.

Did I place you on a pedestal?
The ire of who I wished to be?
Did I vet the situation before I held the key?

You can say you were there,
You can give me shiny things,
But nothing will compare,
To the hurt the ache the sting.

The knowing what had happened,
Will never be erased,
It is over now,
Freedom I will taste.

I did my best to know you.
You did your best to forget me.
In my darkest times bound to your streets,
I won't regret me.

Tiny Dancer

Tiny dancer, you lost your light.
Who hurt you enough to break you?
One day you held music in your mind,
And now your eyes take inventory.
Tiny dancer, who took your story?

So dance, dance tiny dancer.
Dance, dance till you heal her.

Sweet angel, you look afraid.
Who took your solace and your peace?
One day you held memories in your mind,
And now you live to forget.
Who made you regret?

So dance, dance tiny dancer,
Dance dance till you free her.

Do you blame yourself for this feeling?
Your old self is reeling.
Love one another as I have loved you,
But I love them more than me

So dance, dance tiny dancer,
Dance, dance till you heal her.

Dance, dance tiny dancer,
Dance dance till you free her.

Clerical Contemporary

Written like a scrapbook,
Pieced together like summertime ice,
Promises broken like glass in a storm,
I drowned in the contemporary vice,
The clerical noise,
Of hope,
Because that is all I had to call my own.

I can do nice things for you,
I can't do nice things for me,
Because you made me feel unworthy of the best
parts of me,
The parts you took for free,
Are gone.

Who are you?
Who is she?
I once found solace here and now you have
turned my reality to the same dust, you call
reconstruction,
I call destruction.
Now I am without.

I am a clerical contemporary,
Found the modern, lost in the pages,

Everything about this makes me ask what rage
is,
Because I feel heat in my face that I conceal,
From a valley of disappointment,
You won't disappoint me anymore.

You will only be a memory lost to the pages of
this clerical contemporary,
As I turn to a blank epiphany,
Where I piece together the ink of me,
To rewrite my story.

I Think It Broke Me

I walk away appearing to hold on,
The free fall of letting go,
She bit her tongue for so long,
She forgot how to say no.

I think it broke me.

Little miss shiny under pressure,
Finally succumbs to her fate,
The guilt of staying,
The guilt of not being able to wait.

I think they broke me.

Here are the pieces I could find,
I waited too long to be whole,
Just an unfinished diamond lost in a mine,
Searching for the me they stole.

I think I broke me.

Now every time my mind rewinds,
I remember their features,
But their memory I bury deep down,
So I don't ruin my future.

I think they broke me.
I think it broke me.

Let Me Go

You once said you loved me, isn't that so?
Do you love me enough to let me go?
Hold on tight.
Let me go.
I don't know which way to go?
If I stay or if I go,
My love for you is to real to know,
If I should let you go.
As summer's before winter, with autumn left in
tow,
Darling, do you love me, enough to let me go?
My greatest fear is realised,
That you may never know,
My countless years of unrest,
I never let you go.
Hold on tight.
Let me go.
I don't know which way to go?
If I stay or if I go,
But clarity beguiles me,
Once blind now I know,
That you love me enough,
To let me go.
Let me go.
I let you go.
Let you go.

The Darkest Corner

The walls they meet.
The walls enclose.
I walked to the door,
And ran from its' throws.

I danced in the joy that was predisposed,
To me retreating,
I found my repose.

He pulled me from the corner,
I buried myself in.
The corner that haunts me when I'm left in the
din.

The corner that I felt oh so trapped in,
Was left broken,
The door left open,
Standing stuck between virtue and sin.

Is it wrong to want to walk?
Is it wrong to want to run?
Is it wrong to want to go?
Is it wrong to say no?

And the sin of selfishness dissolved into
understanding,
A God so great could never demand me,
To command me, remand me,
To stay there, in the darkest corner.

For it is not wrong to want to run,
When you can no longer walk.
It is not wrong to say no,
When you can no longer talk.
It is not wrong for goodbye,
To come after hello.
It is not wrong to lean on those,
Who reignites your glow.

The light at the end of the tunnel is in front of
you if you turn around,
Look out of the darkest corner onto the hallowed
ground,
A change of perspective does a lot for the soul,
A change of direction can reclaim what they
stole.

When She Is Done

When she is done she holds no animosity,
Her mind cleared like a slate in a violent river,
Eyes focused on the horizon,
Her conviction is as strong as a rock lodged in
Earth's crust,
Bending and breaking in relationship to the
changes that have forged her in fire.

She feels fear, but only around those who truly
know her,
Who can't break her down any more,
For she must repair and regrow her light in the
darkness she encountered,
She must find herself again.
When she is done, there is no undoing her
stance.
Her foot is out the door and her heart is guarded.
To say she feels nothing is a lie,
For she felt everything that brought her to this
moment.
But she won't continue to feel anything for them.
And in this in-between,
Between chaos and the love that frees her,
She is done.

Kaleidoscope

Prisms of colour envelop me,
The rainstorm has halted and bowed to me,
Wrapping me,
Holding me,
Shaping and moulding me.

I danced in the mud,
Without shoes on my feet,
My white dress discoloured,
They called it dirty.

But prismatic colours reflected my skin,
Reminding me of light that I held from within.

In my world, I found my prism,
The kaleidoscope within has risen,
My light reflects the sun and stars,
And they can no longer prod my scars.

In the white dress,
Covered in mud,
I stare at the torn seams,
The tears, sweat, and blood.

All wiped away and renewed in the sun,
My kaleidoscope colours have finally won.

Lightning

I have waited for so long,
Too long to tell you how I feel,
But I wanted to make it real,
So come,
With me to the shoreline.
Hold onto my hand,
And look up at the sky.

I threw lightning,
And it made thunder.
The waves rolled over,
You pulled me under.

I felt the current,
Drank in the sea,
Just me and you,
You and me,
So come,
With me to the shoreline.
Hold onto my hand,
And look up at the sky.

We danced in the ocean,
With sand at our feet.
Until the shoreline did our eyes meet.

Your sunkissed skin, can you feel the heat,
because I threw lightning?

I threw lightning,
And it made thunder.
The waves rolled over,
You pulled me under.

Yes, I threw lightning,
Isn't it bright?
Immersed in the water,
Drowned in starlight.
Now we can be.
So come,
With me to the shoreline.

Beautiful Nothing

O my beautiful nothing,
O my handsome something,
How can mirrors lie,
How can you lie next to I?

O my beautiful heartbreak,
O my handsome heartbeat,
You fall with my tears,
You rise with my dreams,
Your eyes wipe away my fears,
And nothing is as it seems.

O my beautiful nothing,
How can I see you each mirror,
Each light stained reflection,
Each starlit protection,
Against the dark of night,
I hide.

It is not in the frightened,
It is not in the enlightened,
For if it was I would be,
Closer to you my love,
Than you could ever be to me.

My heart feels torn,
My mind feels worn,
For emotion can only hide,
When you are not by my side.

And now I see the night,
And now I see the day,
I see the sun,
I see the stars,
I see the tears,
I feel the scars,
I feel the beginning,
I know not the end,
But each heartbeat quickens,
Before it ends,
I see the present,
I see the past,
I know this moment,
I wish it to last,
For the rivers I have cried,
For the pain that you have felt,
For the ache my heart knows,
It knows also the sweet sting of love,
That comes with sharing suffering,
That comes with understanding loss,
That comes with accepting what you do not
always seek.

And at that moment all I can see is the sun,
All I can see are the stars,
All I can see are the tears,
All I feel are the scars.
The beautiful,
The handsome,
The pretty,
The ugly,
The scars.
They dig deeper than a knife,
But you remind me they don't have to suffocate,
They don't have to strangle,

And in that breath I take a step into the
unknown,

Into the future,
I kiss the sun,
I embrace the starlight,
And for once,
I live.

Honeycomb

Your eyes are a mask no one will see out of and
that you will never see into,
Yet, you know me.

It is as if you understand the intricate
honeycomb of my mind,
And I will be forever free in the land of milk and
honey.

With sapphire lights and endless nights,
Touched by the stars above me,
I danced with joy,
A smile coy,
In the land of milk and honey.

The dawn awakes,
The night foresakes,
From the river to the sea,
For each honeycomb deserves a home,
In the land of milk and honey.

My Angel

I know that I am the only thing holding me back,
I know that you are the only thing pushing me
forward,
And together we meet in the present.
Hold me high when I push me low,
Be my strength when I struggle to swim,
Be my daylight when my joy grows dim,
Be my breath when my heart hurts to beat,
And in your arms let me retreat.
My battle with myself is one I fight each day,

And you love me, but the person you love hurts
the person you adore,

And it hurts me to know I can't take it anymore.

So, I reached my hand out and you took it
regardless of the demons I fight,

You took my hand dragging me out of the night.

And as I opened my eyes to the light of day it
hurt to know that I was the only thing in my
way,

And you fought the me I could not fight,

You fought the anger, the pain and fear so that
my eyes could for once see clear.

You fought for me when I fought you away,
For it hurt too much to watch you stay.
How could you deal with my war?
My mindless ramblings on who knows what for,

My empty tears the pain and hurt,
That I hoped you would just desert.

But you stuck by me as I faced the battle that I
did not want to fight,
Carrying me from the dark into daylight.

A Lover's Gift

Love I wish but love,
And in this wish let no vile stain erase.
The love to you I give,
Breathless though the race.

Heart, I give my heart,
Let no one diminish its beat,
And in its cadence please retreat.

Soul, I give my soul,
Keep it with your own,
Fuse them in our struggle,
Never again to stand alone.

Smile, I give my smile,
And tears if you must cry,
Let me cause your joy,
Sweet surrender, let me try.

Life, I give my life,
My present in your eyes,
And whatever past or future,
To our present love complies.

My Burgundy

I took the quiet,
Traded the silent.
For you and I.

I took the chaos,
Reckoned with loss,
As you stand by.

And while all I do I question,
I never once questioned you.

Like a shadow you danced in time with me,
Like an unplanned orchestra our music echoed
on deaf ears,
But was ours despite the inattention.

I never needed their approval nor begged for
their adoration,
I only asked for our music to keep reminiscing
in my mind.

And like fine wine it grew in passion over time.
Like notes of wood and symphonic burgundy.

Now I lay here drunk on my love for you,
Unable to see the world in the same melancholy
way.
As you whisper things your breath tickles my
ear,
And causes my body to involuntarily sway.

Away to a world where your burgundy dances in
line with my heart,
Pulsing through my veins sweet burgundy my
lifeblood.

For at the end of the dawn and the beginning of
twilight,
I see but one.
I taste but one.
I feel but one.
You are the one.
My one.
My burgundy.

Your Name

Hey there darlin with the wandering smile,
Come over and sit down,
Stay for awhile.

I'll give you today,
If you give your tomorrow.
Maybe my love will drown out your sorrow?

Hey sweet candy,
Your sugar is nectar.
My flower is blooming in your field.
Take me away to your secret garden,
Where summers are endless,
And tomorrow, unreal.

Can I ask this?
Can I say?
I love you my lover.
Tomorrow. Today.
So will you let me take you through the storms
and winding roads,
I will not forsake you, I will take you home.

Can I ask this?
Can I say?

I love you my lover.
Tomorrow. Today.
From the moment I saw you,
I was never the same.
My final breath will be your name.

In My Sometimes

Sometimes life is good. Sometimes life is bad.
Sometimes heartaches turn to breaks and we
hold onto things we shouldn't have.
Sometimes summer is jaded with the ice of
December,
And spring is a fleeting feeling we yearn to
remember.

Sometimes we laugh. Sometimes we cry.
For each day we live is one less we die.
And the hours we spend wrestling with why,
Are minutes we lost like tides that run dry.

That love we chase begins to be clearer,
The closer we get the love it grows dearer,
Until we can touch the love, kiss and hear her,
On whispers of love that reflect in a mirror.

The wrinkles of time etched in her brow,
Bring comfort of years passed until now,
The solace of memory remains here somehow,
The soul, it knows things the mind won't allow.

For sometimes we know, and sometimes we
fade.

The skin on our face, our masquerade.
Sometimes all we have left are memories made,
Living out sometimes alone in the shade,
Living out sometimes for sometimes she stayed.

The Epitaph

Life is a precious thing,
A simple glow of time,
Creating intersections,
As lives, they intertwine.

Hearts grow, break, and beat,
Until one day life's left behind,
And you leave all your intersections,
Reminiscent of your time.

The goal of life is simple,
To make each day matter more.
As each wrinkle and grey hair,
Tallies up your score.

And you look around at the family you created,
Borne from all the intersections where you
patiently waited.

The family that you loved,
Will continue with you in mind,
Stopping at intersections on their own pathways
of time.
Carrying forward your memory knowing fully
well,

That you will live on in stories that time will
surely tell.

www.ingramcontent.com/pod-product-compliance
Lightning Source LLC
Chambersburg PA
CBHW071233140726
47996CB00007B/2586